Engaging Change

The DNA of Modernization

This publication is for the exclusive use of CDER. No part of this book may be reproduced or transmitted in any form or by any means, electronic or mechanical, including photocopying, recording or by any information storage and retrieval system, without written permission from the author, except for the inclusion of brief quotations in a review.
ISBN: 978-1725607873

JIM PEAL, PHD

CHARLOTTE MILLINER, MS
A course presented by
The Center for Professional Development, Inc.

CDER use only

Notes

Focus for today

Engaging Change

- Dynamics of change
- Approaching change
    - Positive and Negative Intent & Attitudes
- Building strengths and resiliency
- Robust communication skills
- Introduction to: Modernizing FDA's New Drugs Regulatory Program
- Three conversations – model & practice
    - Talking about Change
        - Framing the positives
    - Frequent Check-ins
        - 2 questions
        - On-going collaboration
    - Coaching
        - For support and when issues arise

A Strong Foundation Expands Great Results

{ **Accomplishments** }

- Actions
- Agreements
- Alignment
- Trust and Partnership

Results and Accomplishments Expand

A Strong Foundation Expands Great Results

Foundation of Trust and Partnership

Operate from Leadership Strengths
Know the people that you work with
Strengths – what makes you/them feel strong
Communication Style
Work style
Sustained Quality Communication

Trust and Partnership

EQ-i Model of Emotional Intelligence

Fifteen dimensions of human nature

Personal
Unknown to Others
Known to Self

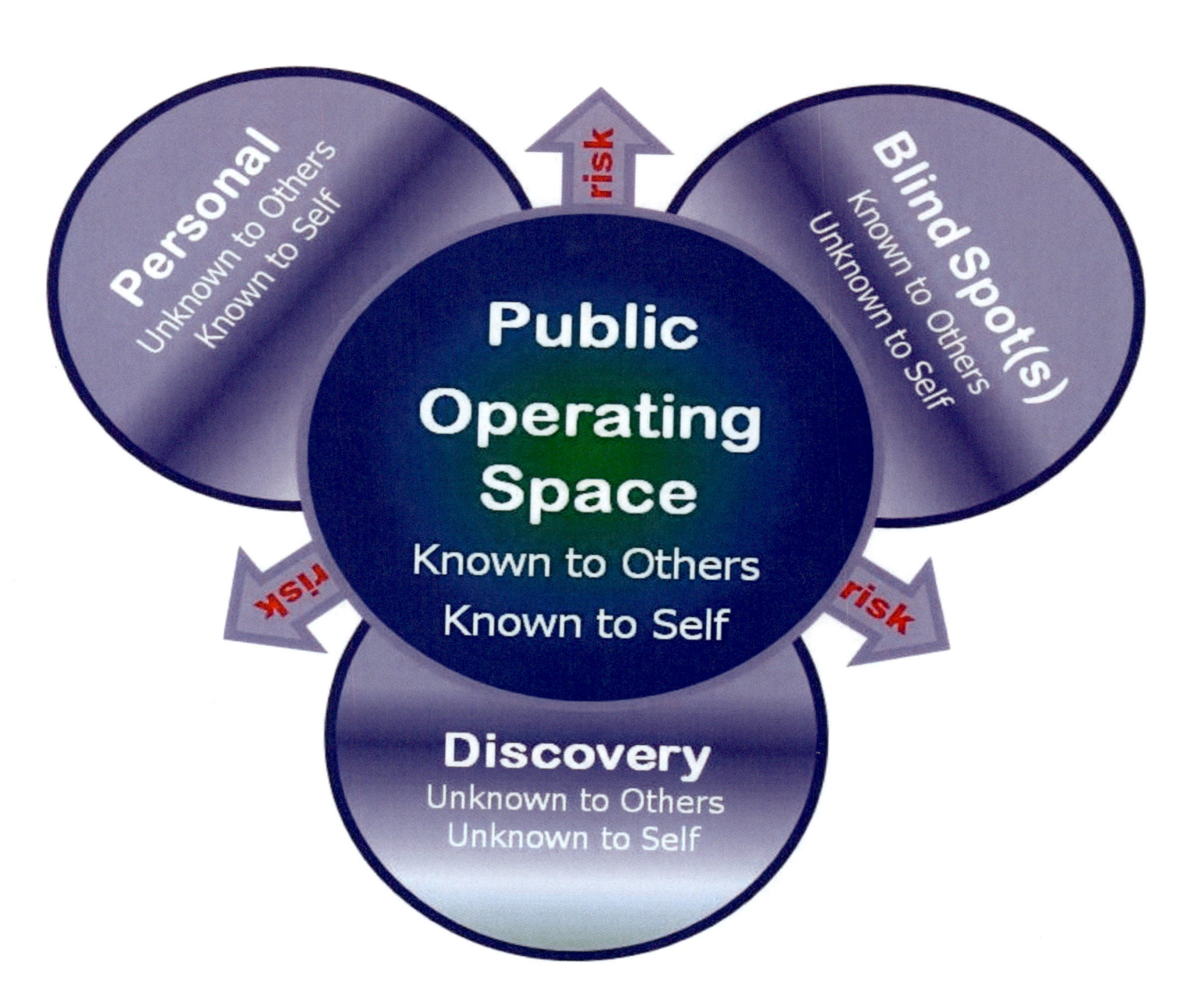

Blind Spot(s)
Known to Others
Unknown to Self

Public Operating Space
Known to Others
Known to Self

Discovery
Unknown to Others
Unknown to Self

risk

What does your attitude have to do with engaging and implementing change?

Your energy is contagious.

Either you affect people or you infect people.

The choice is yours.

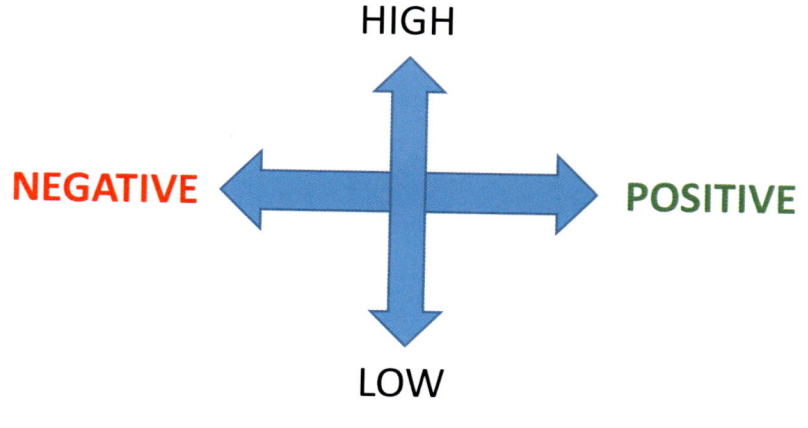

```
          HIGH
           ↑
NEGATIVE ←─┼─→ POSITIVE
           ↓
          LOW
```

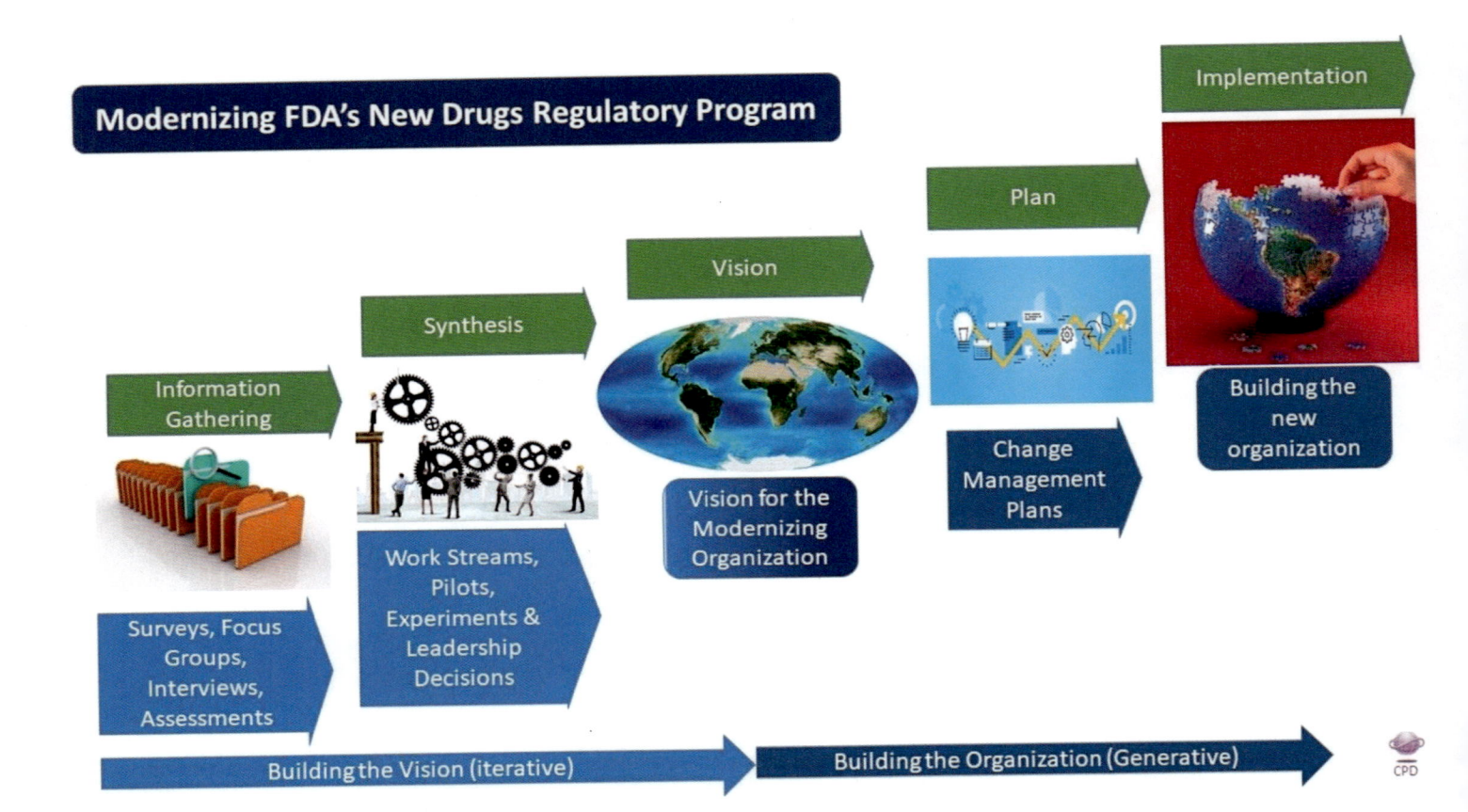

Modernization Overview

Modernizing FDA's New Drugs Regulatory Program

Information Gathering → **Synthesis** → **Vision** → **Plan** → **Implementation**

- Surveys, Focus Groups, Interviews, Assessments
- Work Streams, Pilots, Experiments & Leadership Decisions
- Vision for the Modernizing Organization
- Change Management Plans
- Building the new organization

Building the Vision (iterative) → Building the Organization (Generative)

GO TO SharePoint   http://sharepoint.fda.gov/orgs/CDER-OND-CI/

NEW DRUGS PROGRAM WORKSTREAMS AND PILOTS

D Workstreams overview

Workstreams

OND Clinical Structure	Peter Stein, Hylton Joffe, Mary Thanh-Hai	Evaluating current distribution and workload trends across Divisions and therapeutic areas to understand the optimal future state structure
IO Realignment/New Drug Policy Office	Peter Stein, Patrick Frey, Keith Flanagan	Designing the transition state organization for the IO to provide clear ownership and support for operations, drug development and policy
Regulatory Operations	Patrick Frey	Focusing on improvements to the capabilities, tools, and structure of Regulatory Operations to elevate the project management discipline
Pre-Market Safety Assessment	Peter Stein	Identifying and piloting initiatives to improve NDA/BLA safety reviews by developing consistent approaches and clear roles & responsibilities
Pre-Market Assessment Process	Peter Stein	Designing a consistent approach to NDA/BLA reviews focused on reducing redundancy and ensuring high-quality reviews
IND Content	Peter Stein/ Hylton Joffe	Improving the efficiency and quality of the IND scientific and clinical content; initial focus on 30 Day Safety Reviews and Protocols
IND Process	Patrick Frey	Reviewing the current state of IND processes to align and implement initiatives to improve processes and drive consistency throughout OND
Documentation [Phase 1 & 2]	John Farley	Identifying and prioritizing OND document stakeholder needs to develop and pilot new standard review documentation and tools
Assessing Talent	Theresa Mullin	Developing a new interview and assessment process for candidates for clinical roles and a performance evaluation process for 1st years

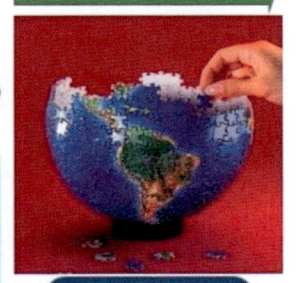

Modernizing FDA's New Drugs Regulatory Program

Information Gathering → Synthesis → Vision → Plan → Implementation

Surveys, Focus Groups, Interviews, Assessments → Work Streams, Pilots, Experiments & Leadership Decisions → Vision for the Modernizing Organization → Change Management Plans → Building the new organization

Building the Vision (iterative) → **Building the Organization (Generative)**

CPD

Specific plans will be sent to you

Quarterly Newsletter will be sent to you

GO TO SharePoint   http://sharepoint.fda.gov/orgs/CDER-OND-CI/

Notes

The Change Curve

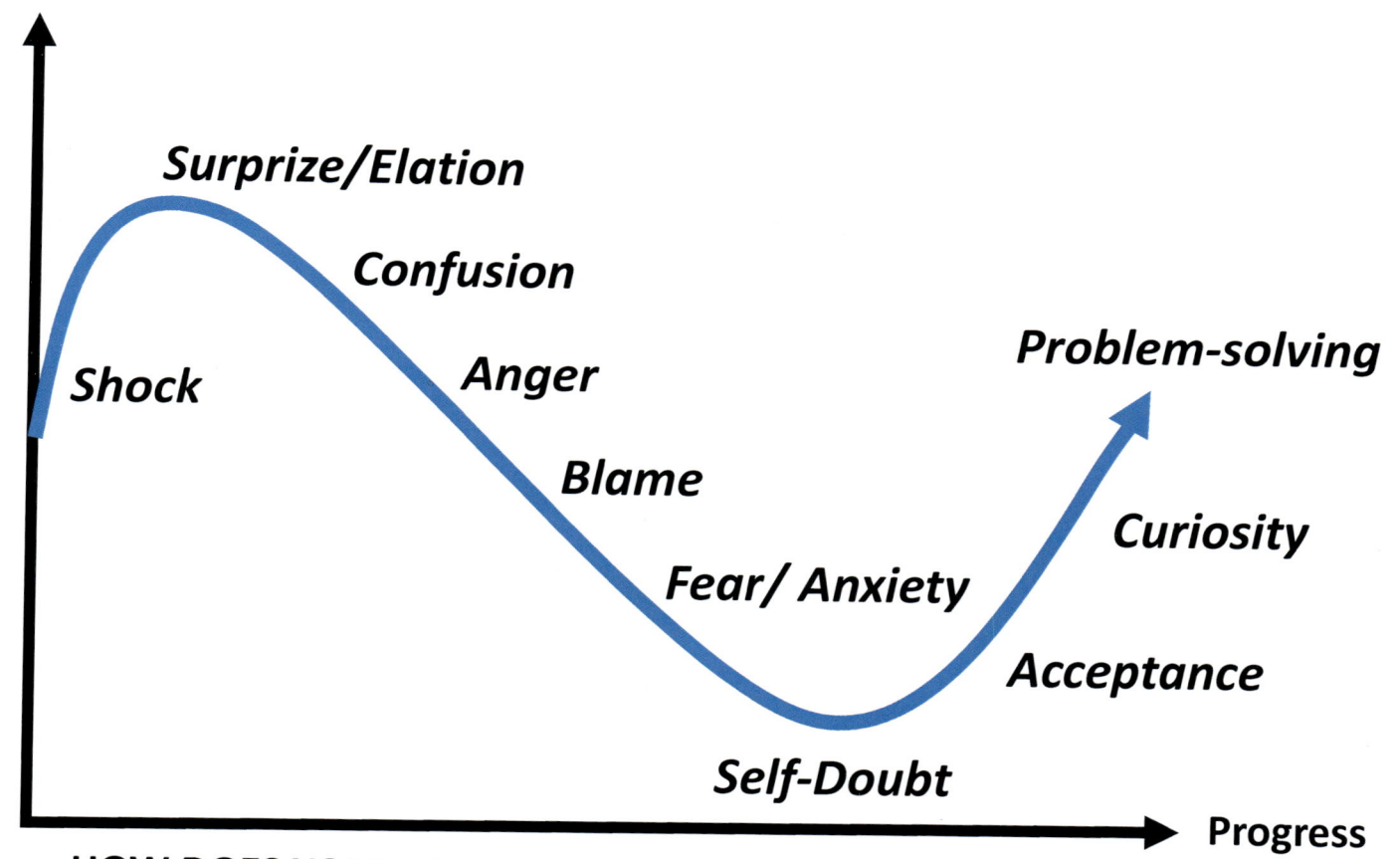

Performance & Self-Esteem ↑

- Shock
- Surprize/Elation
- Confusion
- Anger
- Blame
- Fear/Anxiety
- Self-Doubt
- Acceptance
- Curiosity
- Problem-solving

→ Progress

HOW DOES YOUR EXPERIENCE RELATE TO THIS MODEL?

Adapted from Kubler-Ross

Hanlon's Paradox:
"Impending or actual change lowers self-esteem and the ability to cope with change just at the time we most need it."

Check Your Tude®

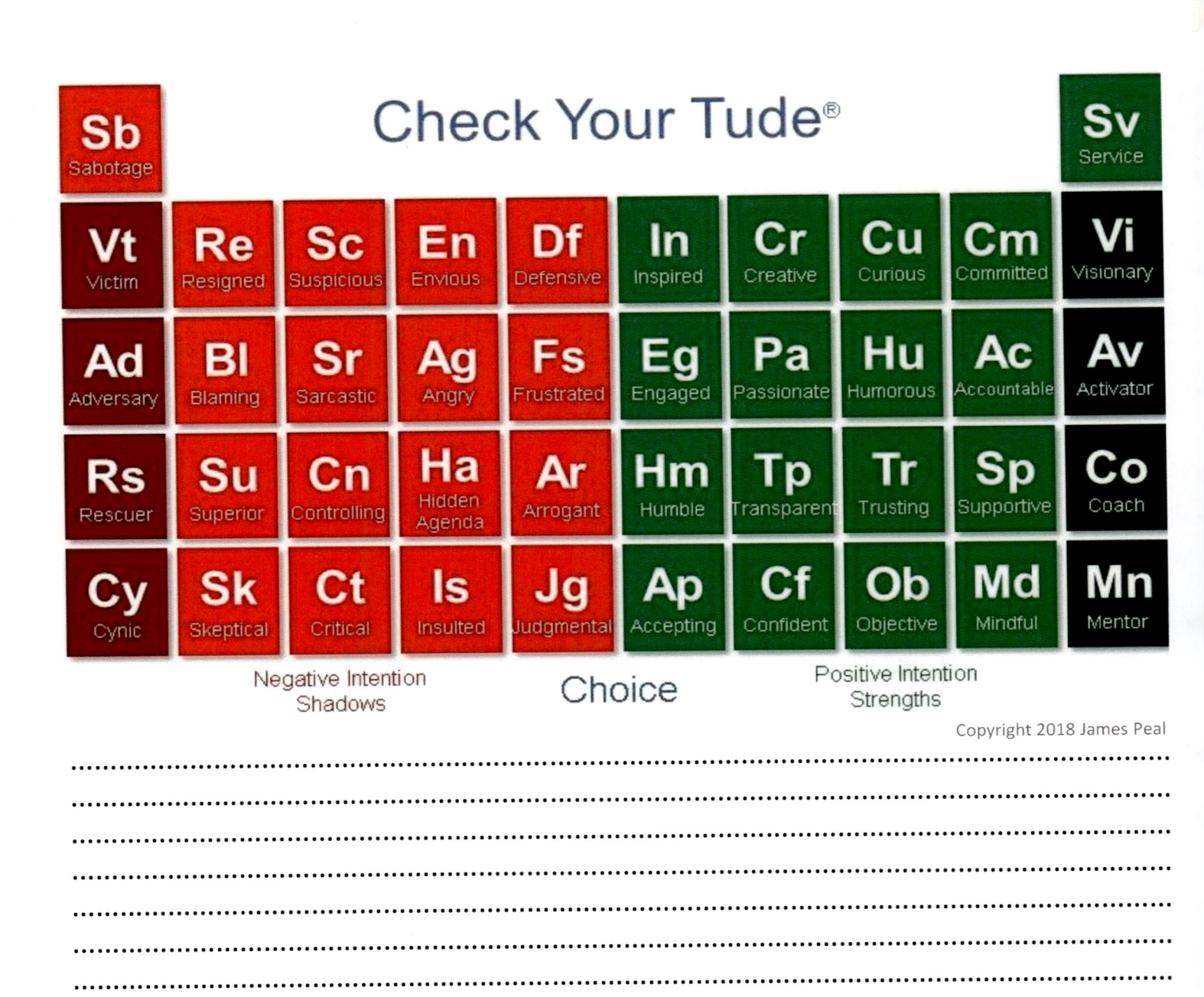

Sb Sabotage										Sv Service
Vt Victim	Re Resigned	Sc Suspicious	En Envious	Df Defensive	In Inspired	Cr Creative	Cu Curious	Cm Committed	Vi Visionary
Ad Adversary	Bl Blaming	Sr Sarcastic	Ag Angry	Fs Frustrated	Eg Engaged	Pa Passionate	Hu Humorous	Ac Accountable	Av Activator
Rs Rescuer	Su Superior	Cn Controlling	Ha Hidden Agenda	Ar Arrogant	Hm Humble	Tp Transparent	Tr Trusting	Sp Supportive	Co Coach
Cy Cynic	Sk Skeptical	Ct Critical	Is Insulted	Jg Judgmental	Ap Accepting	Cf Confident	Ob Objective	Md Mindful	Mn Mentor

Negative Intention Shadows   Choice   Positive Intention Strengths

Copyright 2018 James Peal

....
....
....
....
....
....
....

Plot Your Change Journey

Performance & Self-Esteem

Progress

Plot your key primary attitudes along the graph along with the Green attitude that enhances your effectiveness

The Glass is ½ Full

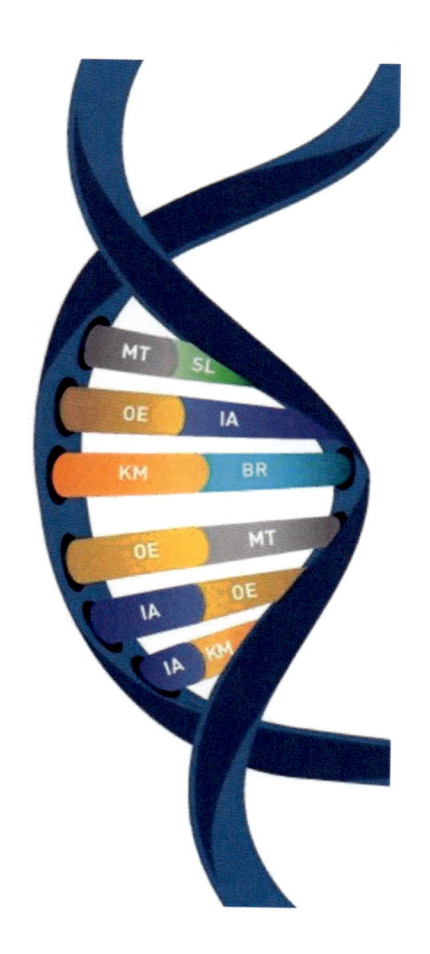

- Review the document
- Scan for what you like about what you are reading
- Write notes about what you like about the program
- What can you say about the Modernization that:
    - Acknowledges past excellence
    - We are world leaders
    - Room for improvement
    - Personal - positive tone/emotion/heart felt/excited/passion
    - Show what you are bought into and why
    - Examples of problems where we need to change
    - It will take work and will be worth it
    - WIIFM – What's in it for me/us

Notes

"The patients we serve trust us to do our job. They enroll in clinical trials because they know we are watching over them. They take approved drugs because they know they meet our standards. They report side effects because they know we will seriously explore them. Because people trust us, we're asked to do more and more. But we can't just work harder to keep up. To maintain and advance our global leadership - and better support our deeply committed staff - we need to modernize the New Drugs Regulatory Program."

Janet Woodcock, M.D.,
Director, Center for Drug Evaluation and Research (CDER),
and Acting Director, Office of New Drugs (OND)

KEY CHALLENGES

The New Drugs Regulatory Program reacts to PDUFA submissions in a timely and predictable manner. We also need to be proactive leaders on behalf of the people we serve.

Our ecosystem is evolving rapidly. We face growing stakeholder engagement and expectations, new science and technology, health care system cost constraints, and a growing CDER workload. These trends are expected to intensify. Our program was not designed with these challenges in mind. To maintain and advance our global leadership, the New Drugs Regulatory Program must adapt and evolve.

Growing stakeholder engagement and expectations. Patients are providing more input on meaningful endpoints and benefit-risk determinations. Thanks to the 21st Century Cures Act and PDUFA VI, we are integrating a patient focus into regulatory decision-making. We are expected to play a major role in developing the next generation of drug development tools - including patient reported outcomes, biomarkers, and clinical outcome assessments - and in accelerating drug development generally. At the same time, industry is globalizing, multiple drug regulatory authorities around the world are maturing, and stakeholders expect more transparency from FDA.

New science and technology. Rapid scientific advances are enhancing understanding of disease pathologies. New types of drugs target diseases in new ways. Combination products create new delivery methods. There is an increasing emphasis on precision medicine, rare diseases, and defined subsets of common diseases. We must adapt to new data sources and technologies, such as Real World Evidence and "big data."

Health care system cost constraints and a growing CDER workload. The health care system is coping with substantial cost pressures. To manage drug costs, payors are focusing on generics, biosimilars, new products with differentiated therapeutic value, and repurposed approved drugs. Drug developers are also innovating to reduce the cost and time of drug development. Patients struggle with high drug costs. CDER's workload is growing. We are implementing multiple unfunded or partially-funded Congressional mandates. 41% of CDER employees and 45% of OND employees say their workload is unreasonable.

Modernizing FDA's New Drugs Regulatory Program:
STRATEGIC OBJECTIVES

The New Drugs Regulatory Program includes the Office of New Drugs, the Office of Translational Sciences, the Office of Surveillance and Epidemiology, the Office of Pharmaceutical Quality, and other parts of FDA.

Modernization of the New Drugs Regulatory Program will be a long-term process of continuous improvement, not a sudden event. Modernization will focus on six strategic objectives:

Scientific Leadership [SL]

We will grow our scientific expertise and clarify pathways to regulatory approval.

Expanding the armamentarium to address unmet medical needs is an important part of our public health mission. Toward that end, we will proactively collaborate with academic medical scientists and patient/disease advocates, evaluate scientific gaps, and strategically foster drug development.

Integrated Assessment [IA]

We will critically, collaboratively, and consistently assess whether information in submissions meets statutory and regulatory requirements.

We will take a new approach to document our assessments, developing a more integrated, cross-disciplinary document to foster collaboration and reduce redundant information. Our assessments will be rigorous, risk-based, and clinically relevant; focus on the issues; and consider the patient perspective.

Benefit-Risk Monitoring [BR]

We will establish a unified post-market safety surveillance framework.

To effectively protect the American public, we will systematically monitor the benefits and risks of approved drugs across their lifecycles.

Managing Talent [MT]

We will attract, develop, and retain outstanding people.

We will use 21st Century Cures Act authorities to recruit and retain technical, scientific, and professional experts, and eliminate our backlog of vacant positions.

Operational Excellence [OE]

We will have a dedicated focus on operational excellence.

We will standardize workflow, roles, and responsibilities to improve operational efficiency, and enable our scientists to focus on science, not ancillary tasks. For example, within OND, we will consolidate administrative, regulatory project management, policy, and drug development tools teams. These teams will provide direct support to OND offices and divisions. Certain offices and divisions will be clustered to better reflect current and emerging understanding of disease, and review teams will remain strongly intact.

Knowledge Management [KM]

We will facilitate knowledge management.

Vast and diverse information is submitted to and generated by FDA's New Drugs Regulatory Program. We will make it easy for our staff to find and use scientific and regulatory precedents, reducing manual work time, increasing the speed and efficiency of submission assessment, and increasing the consistency and predictability of regulatory decision-making.

Check-In Conversation

Frequent strengths based conversations about near term future work

5-7minutes long

What are your priorities this week? How can I help you?

Notes

Notes

Best Practices Communication Skills

{ **Acknowledgement** }

Clean-Up

Discuss Real Issues

Assume Positive Intention

Notes

Check Your Attitude Coaching

The steps to become aware of your negative limiting mindsets and shift to a positive and productive mindset.

1. What are your **Positive Intention Strengths**?
2. What situation/person triggers you to go into a **Negative Intention Shadow**?
    - Where do you go?
    - What is the thought or conclusion that starts you spinning?
3. Step into **Choice Point**. Pause for a moment.
    - Take a few breaths to clear your emotional palette and calm your thoughts.
4. What **Positive Intention Strengths** would be useful in this situation?
    - Play the situation in your mind from your **Positive Intention Strengths**.
    - What difference does it make in how you think, feel and act?
5. What **reminder/anchor** can you put in place to shift yourself quickly to your **Positive Intention Strengths** next time?

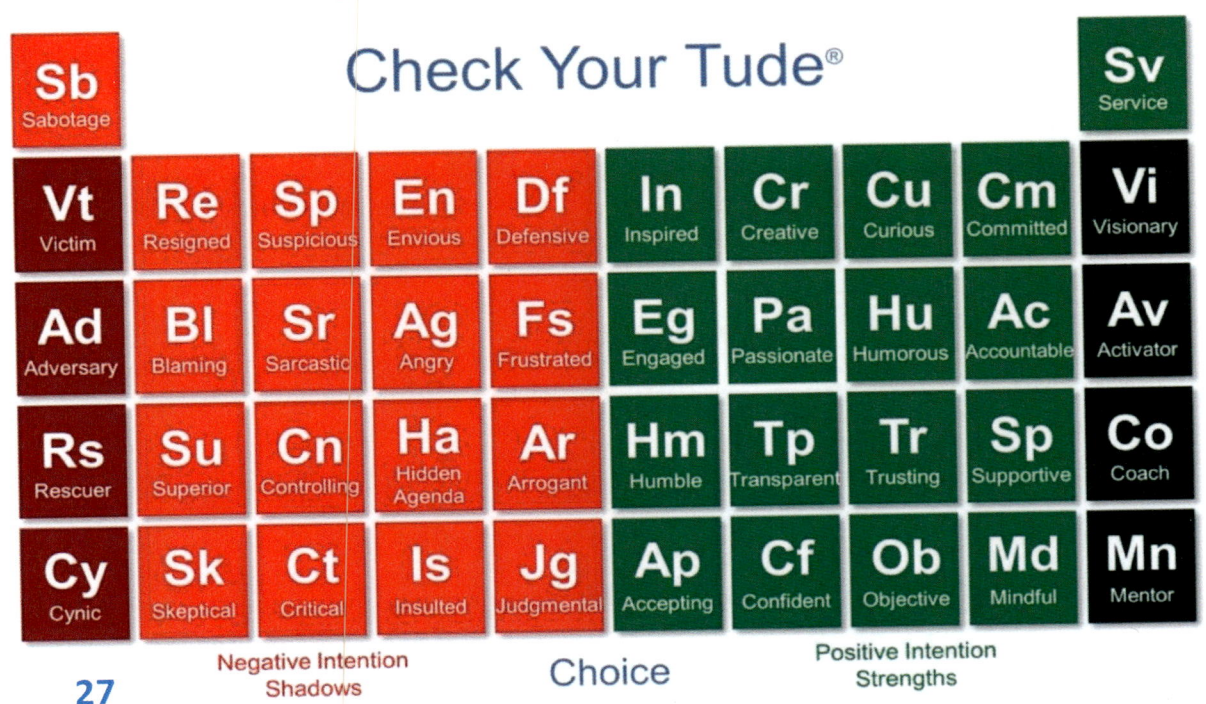

Check Your Tude®

Sb Sabotage										Sv Service
Vt Victim	Re Resigned	Sp Suspicious	En Envious	Df Defensive	In Inspired	Cr Creative	Cu Curious	Cm Committed	Vi Visionary	
Ad Adversary	Bl Blaming	Sr Sarcastic	Ag Angry	Fs Frustrated	Eg Engaged	Pa Passionate	Hu Humorous	Ac Accountable	Av Activator	
Rs Rescuer	Su Superior	Cn Controlling	Ha Hidden Agenda	Ar Arrogant	Hm Humble	Tp Transparent	Tr Trusting	Sp Supportive	Co Coach	
Cy Cynic	Sk Skeptical	Ct Critical	Is Insulted	Jg Judgmental	Ap Accepting	Cf Confident	Ob Objective	Md Mindful	Mn Mentor	

Negative Intention Shadows | Choice | Positive Intention Strengths

Notes

GROW Coaching

- **G**OAL
  - What is the goal you are trying to reach?
- **R**EALITY
  - Where are you today in regards to your goal?
- **O**PTIONS
  - What are your options to get there?
  - What have you tried already?
- **W**AY FORWARD
  - What are your next steps?

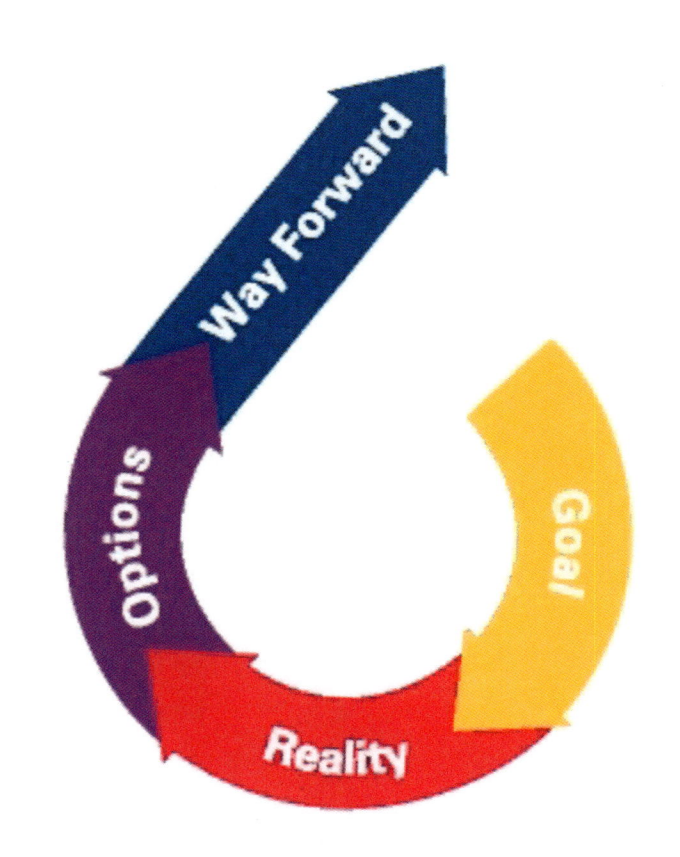

Made in the USA
Columbia, SC
08 October 2018